STORIES BY TERAMURA TERUO

Japanese "Characters"
A COLLECTION OF GRADED READERS
FOR STUDENTS OF JAPANESE

ELEMENTARY

1 Stories by Teramura Teruo (1992)

INTERMEDIATE

4 Stories by Tsubota Jōji (1992)

ADVANCED

9 "Chickens" by Mori Ōgai (1992)

Japanese "Characters"

GRADED READERS: ELEMENTARY

1

Stories by Teramura Teruo

translated by

Edmund R. Skrzypczak

JAPAN PUBLICATIONS TRADING CO., LTD.
TOKYO, JAPAN

© 1992 by Edmund R. Skrzypczak (English translation)
English translation rights arranged with Rironsha, Tokyo, Japan.

Published by JAPAN PUBLICATIONS TRADING CO., LTD.
1-2-1, Sarugaku-chō, Chiyoda-ku,
Tokyo, 101 Japan

Original Japanese language edition © 1975 by Teruo Teramura and
Shizuko Wakayama, published by Rironsha, Tokyo, Japan.

Distributors:
UNITED STATES & CANADA: *JP Trading, Inc., P. O. BOX 610,
300 Industrial Way, Brisbane, CA 94005.*
BRITISH ISLES & EUROPEAN CONTINENT: *Premier Book Marketing Ltd.,
1 Gower Street, London WC1E 6HA.*
AUSTRALIA & NEW ZEALAND: *Bookwise International, 54 Crittenden
Road, Findon, South Australia 5023.*
THE FAR EAST & JAPAN: *Japan Publications Trading Co., Ltd.,
1-2-1, Sarugaku-chō, Chiyoda-ku, Tokyo, 101 Japan.*

First edition: July 1992 (First printing)

ISBN 0-87040-914-X

Printed in Japan

Contents

About the Series

Tens of thousands of people around the world are now studying Japanese as a foreign language. University departments that offer Japanese are experiencing an unprecedented boom. Japanese is being taught in more and more high schools, and even in primary schools in some parts of the world.

Regardless of their ages, there comes a point when these language students would like to read something in Japanese. If they are beginners, or sometimes even if they have been studying Japanese for two or three years, they still do not know enough kanji to be able to read ordinary books in Japanese. Or, even if the book is mostly in kana, they find the vocabulary too much of a problem. Thus, whether it be kanji that is the obstacle, or vocabulary, their desire to read is frustrated.

The books in this series are designed to meet the needs of such students. They will bridge the gap between the classroom and the library (or bookshop). They will also, I believe, help students consolidate what they learn in the classroom, because stories about situations that can be easily imagined provide tangible examples of words, phrases, and grammatical structures being used in specific contexts. These examples leave deep impressions on the imagination and memory of the reader.

I have tried as much as possible to make the English translation pass muster as English. More important to me, however, was capturing the sense and feeling of the original Japanese, since the idea of having a translation opposite the Japanese text is to aid the student to understand the original. Sometimes capturing the sense of the original meant choosing an English turn of expression that is far from a literal translation of the Japanese, yet is what would be (or could be) used in English to convey the same meaning. After all, the expression, the communication, of meaning is what language is all about, and the reader should learn to grasp the meaning of what is being read.

It is always a problem when devising a series of books such as this, to imagine who the readers will be. Will they be university students? high-school students? second-year students of the language? third-year students? Et cetera. At first I planned to assume that the potential reader would have studied Japanese for two years using one of Anthony Alfonso's structured textbooks, because then I would know, roughly, what vocabulary, grammar, and kanji the reader would have learned. But in view of the enormous boom in Japanese language study in recent years, with the subsequent proliferation of textbooks and diversity in teaching approaches, I decided to aim at a very vague type of reader: someone who had learned some Japanese (formally or informally), knew enough kana to get started, and maybe knew no kanji whatsoever—but who wanted something to read.

For this reason, the first book in this series begins with very few kanji, which appear with the kana readings over them. In subsequent books kanji are introduced more frequently, but in such a way as not, I trust, to overburden the reader. The series as a whole will be divided into three levels of difficulty: elementary, intermediate, and advanced, with the number of kanji increasing gradually with each book in the series.

The Japanese stories chosen for inclusion in this series have been selected because they show aspects of Japan or of Japanese people — sometimes even aspects of the authors who wrote the stories — that reveal the Japanese as people. This is important, because the whole key to understanding people of other countries is the realization that, underneath their different appearances and different ways of doing things, they are people, the same as you, the same as the other people you know.

Finally, the stories were also chosen in the hope that they will prove entertaining. This can be a difficult order to fill sometimes, since what is entertaining to me might not be so to everyone else. Still, most people enjoy meeting interesting people, and it is with this in mind that I have aimed at introducing you to some real "characters." Happy reading!

Edmund R. Skrzypczak

Introduction

This first book in the series of graded readers contains two stories by Teramura Teruo in which the main character is a king. Mr Teramura wrote a whole series of books about this king, and at the very beginning of the first book in the series the author made the cryptic remark, "There is a king in every family." If the author is correct, then as you read about the king in these two stories you should keep finding things that vaguely remind you of someone you know.

The author, Mr Teramura Teruo, was born in Tokyo in 1928. A graduate of the Department of Politics and Economics of Waseda University, he now teaches at Bunkyō Women's College in Tokyo, and somehow manages to find the time to write children's stories. He has written many, and many of these have won awards or been designated as recommended reading by the Japanese Library Association. His series of ten books on the king is perhaps his most famous, although, for some little fans of his, his more recent series on "Komatta san" and "Wakatta san" might be more familiar. If you enjoy the stories about the king presented in this first volume of the series, I urge you to try your hand at one of the "Komatta san" books next. In "Komatta san," the energetic young woman who owns the flower shop by the train station, Mr Teramura has created another one of his unforgettable characters. Like Dr Watson in the Sherlock Holmes tales, who spends more time solving crimes than attending patients, "Komatta san" will live longer in our memories for whipping up emergency concoctions in her kitchen than for arranging bouquets.

Though Mr Teramura's king series is aimed at young readers, I know at least one university professor who became addicted to the king stories after he started reading them to his children at bedtime. Adults, therefore, are not immune to becoming "hooked." The plots are clever, the situations are humorous, the language is fresh and lively. You, as a student of the language, will find in these stories a great deal you can imitate and use in your own conversations.

There is a progression in the amount of kanji I introduce in these two stories, with very few throughout most of the first story, and what I consider a light burden of kanji in the second. (The second story, therefore, has a bit more kanji than the author's original; you can find the original stories, by the way, in *Ōsama robotto*, Rironsha,

1975; 45th reprinting, 1988.) Rather than have an invarying, mathematical policy on the *furigana* (the hiragana over the kanji), I put them in when I thought they might be of help to the reader, and when I thought those particular *furigana* had been seen sufficient times already, or given just shortly before, I left them out. If there was any doubt in my mind about whether to put in or leave out, I always chose to put them in.

This book is a reader, not a textbook of grammar. Quite possibly you will come across an expression whose grammatical function you have not learned. If the translation fails to provide enough clues to enlighten you, you will have to consult: a) your language textbook; b) a dictionary of grammar; or c) your teacher — or perhaps all three (why not?). Given the great variety of textbooks in use today, and the disparity in the backgrounds of potential readers of these books, I decided it would be impossible to know which points of grammar needed footnoting. In the hope that the translation itself will serve to make most things clear, I have restricted notes to a bare minimum. Where a note is given, there will be an asterisk (*) in the Japanese text, and the note will appear at the foot of the English translation on the facing page.

Robot Does It All

TERAMURA Teruo

なんでもロボット

　まあきいてください。王さまのはなしなんです。

　朝、七時になると、王さまのおきる時間です。

　　　　テレレッテ　プルルップ

　　　　トロロット　タ　ター

　おしろで、　ラッパがなります。そして、王さまのへ
やに、大臣がやってきます。

「王さま、ラッパがなりましたよ。さあ、おきてくださ
い。」

　大臣がいうと、

「うるさいな。まだ七時じゃないよ。」

「いや、たしかにラッパがなりました。」

「おしろのとけいが、すすんでいるんだ。」

「すすんでいません。あっています。」

「なにをっ。王さまにむかって、なんということを言う
んだ。」

　王さまは、そうさけんで、ベッドの上に立ち上がりま

Robot Does It All

All right, pay attention now. This story's about a king.

Every morning at seven it's rise-and-shine time for the king.

Ta-ta ta-ra-ra, ta-ta ta-rara

Ta-ta ta-rara ta-raa

A bugle blows in the palace. Then the chief minister comes to the king's room.

"Your Majesty, the bugle has sounded. Get up please," he says.

"Don't bother me. It's not seven yet."

"No, no mistake. The bugle has sounded."

"The palace clock is fast, that's why."

"It is not fast, it's right on time."

"What!?! How dare you talk that way to your king!!" cried the king as he stood up in bed.

した。すると、

「王さま、おはようございます。そうら、おきましたね。もう、ねてはいけませんよ。」

　大臣が、わらいながらおじぎをしたので、すっかり目がさめてしまいました。

「……くやしいなあ……」

　王さまは、まるできげんがわるいのです。

「朝は、いつまでもねていたいなあ。そして、夜は、ねむくなったら、ねてしまうんだ……」

　そのとき、王さまの〈かおを洗う時間〉がきました。

「ああ、めんどくさい。わしは、歯をみがくのが、大きらいだ。」

　つぎは、〈ごはんの前の、かるいたいそうの時間〉です。

「ああ、めんどくさい。たいそうなんか、＊　しなくてもいいのにな。」

　おわるとこんどは、〈ごはんの前の、手を洗う時間〉です。

「ああ、めんどくさい。いちいち手なんか洗わなくてもいいのになあ。だれか、かわって、洗ってくれればいいのに……」

　だれか、かわりに――。そうです。王さまは、いいこ

"Good morning, Your Majesty! There, you're up. You mustn't go back to sleep now."

The chief minister bowed to him, a smile on his face. This made the king wide awake.

". . . makes me so mad . . . ." And in a thoroughly bad mood.

"I wish I could sleep as long as I want in the morning. And go to bed at night only when I'm sleepy . . . ."

The king's "Washing-Up Time" had arrived.

"Oh, bother! I hate brushing my teeth."

Next it was "Light-Exercises-Before-Breakfast Time."

"Ooh, bother!! I wish I didn't have to do stupid exercises."

When these were finished, it was "Washing-Hands-Before-Meals Time."

"Oooh, bother!!! I wish I didn't have to wash my darn hands every single time. If only somebody would wash his hands instead of me . . . ."

(Somebody . . . instead . . . . That's it!) The

---

* なんか : lit., "and the like"; here, shows annoyance.

19

とをかんがえました。大臣をよんで、こう言いました。

「わしにそっくりのロボットをつくれ。いま、すぐに
だっ。」

　王さまは、いいだしたらきかないのです。いったい、
そんなロボットが出来るでしょうか。出来なくとも、作
らなければならないのです。

「は、はっ。」

　おしろのはかせは、さっそく、けんきゅうにとりかか
りました。

　王さまは、にやり。

「さあ、ロボットが出来れば、めんどうなことは、みん
なさせてしまえばいい、わしのすることは、ねることと、
食べることだけだ。」

　そこで、王さまの〈朝ごはんの時間〉がはじまりまし
た。

　さて、おしろの中に、王さまがふたり出来ました。

「王さま、〈べんきょうの時間〉です。」

　大臣がよぶと、

king had a bright idea.

Summoning the chief minister, he told him: "Make me a robot that looks exactly like me. Now! At once!"

Once the king says something he won't change his mind. Was such a robot really possible? Well, even if it wasn't, they would have to make one.

"Ye- . . . yes, Your Majesty!"

The palace wise man at once set about studying how to make one.

The king grinned. "When the robot is finished, I can make it do all the irksome things, and all I will have to do is sleep, and eat."

At which point the king's "Breakfast Time" began.

Well, now there were two kings in the palace.

When the chief minister would call, "Your Majesty, it's 'Study Time,'" the real king would

「よろしい。いま、行くぞ。」

　ホンモノの王さまは、そう言って、ロボットをべんきょうのへやに行かせました。えらい先生は、ロボットに、べんきょうをおしえるのです。

　王さまは、ごろごろ　ねころがっています。

「王さま、かみのけがのびました。とこやをしましょう。」

「よろしい、いますぐ、行くぞ。」

　ホンモノの王さまは、そうこたえますが、とこやさんは、ロボットのあたまを、じょきじょき　ちゃっきん。

　王さまは、ごろごろ　ねころがっています。

「王さま、ようふくやがまいりました。あたらしいようふくを作りましょう。」

「よろしい、いますぐ、行くぞ。」

　ようふくやは、ロボットのすんぽうにあわせて、ようふくを作ります。

　王さまは、ごろごろ　ねころがっています。

「王さま、〈うんどうの時間〉です。きょうは、馬のりの日です。」

「ああ、いいとも、すぐによういしろ。」

　ロボットが馬にのると、かっぱ　ぽっこと　走りだしました。

22

say, "Fine, I'm on my way." Then he would send the robot to the study room, where the famous teacher would give the robot lessons.

The king would sprawl out on his couch.

"Your Majesty, your hair has grown. How about a haircut?"

"Fine, I'll go at once," the real king would reply, but the royal barber's scissors would go "snip, snip, *clip*" over the robot's head. The king would be sprawled out on his couch.

"Your Majesty, the tailor has arrived. Let's have him make you a new suit of clothes."

"Fine, I'll be there in a jiff." And the tailor would make a suit of clothes to fit the robot's measurements. The king stayed sprawled on his couch.

"Your Majesty, it's 'Exercise Time.' Today's the day for horseriding."

"Oh yes, good. Prepare the horse at once." The robot mounted the horse and it galloped off,

　王さまはごろごろ　ねころがっています。

　ごろごろ　ねころがって、おきると、おかしを食べて、またねころがって、テレビを見ています。おきあがるのは、ものを食べるときだけなんです。

　ふしぎなことです。

　ロボットは、何をやっても、じょうずなのです。馬にのるのなんて、先生よりじょうずかもしれません。けっして、ころがったりしないのでした。

　ロボットは、べんきょうが大すきでした。こくごも、さんすうも、おんがくも、こうさくも、みんな王さまより、よく出来るのです。先生より、よく出来るかもしれません。けっして、まちがったりしないのでした。

　ロボットは、もんくを言いません。何をやらせても、いやだと言いません。言われたとおり、はい、はい、とやります。

　「おなかが、すいたぞっ。」などと、どなりません。

　「ねむくなったぞっ。」などと、わがままを言いません。

　「あたまがいたい。」などと、ないたりしません。

24

while the king lay sprawled on his couch.

Sprawling on his couch, only getting up to have some sweets, then lying down again, he watched television. The only time he would get up was to eat something.

It was amazing.

Everything the robot did, it did well.

In horseback riding, for example, it was possibly more skilful than the teacher. For it never took a spill.

It loved study. Japanese classes, maths, music, handicrafts . . . in all these subjects it did better than the king. It may have been better than the teacher, even. For it never made a mistake.

And the robot never complained. No matter what it was told to do, it never said "No!" It always answered "Yes, sir!" and did as it was told.

It never roared out anything like "I'm hungry!"

It never tried to have its own way, saying things like "I'm sleepy!"

It never said things like "I have a headache!" and then start crying or the like.

けれども、ホンモノ王さま——。あれから、いちども
かおを洗いません。とこやもしません。ようふくもきた
まま。ただ一日中ごろごろ、おいものように　ごろごろ
ごろごろ、おいものように、どろだらけのきたならしい
王さまになりました。

「王さま、となりの国から、サーカスを見に来ないかと
いう手紙が来ました。」

　大臣が、いいました。

「よし、サーカスには、わしが行くぞ。」

なんでもロボットにやらせる王さまは、このときばかり
は、自分が行くと言いだしました。

「でも……王さま。」

「でも、何だ。」

「王さまと、ロボットをくらべると……」

「くらべると、どうしたんだ。」

「そのままでは、みっともないんじゃありませんか。王
さまは……」

　王さまは、いわれて、自分とロボットをくらべてみま

But the real king, now . . . . Well, once the robot came on the scene, the king didn't wash himself once, didn't shave or have his hair cut, didn't bother to change his clothes. All he did was lie on his couch all day long, like a sack of potatoes. And he became as dirty and filthy as a sack of potatoes.

"Your Majesty, a letter has arrived from our neighbors, inviting you to come see a circus," said the chief minister.

"All right! A circus . . . now that's something I'll go to."

The king was making the robot do everything; this was the only time he proposed to go himself.

"But Your Majesty . . . ."

"But what?"

"If we compare Your Majesty . . . and the robot
. . . ."

"So you compare me and the robot, so what?"

"In Your Majesty's present state, I think you might be a bit unsightly . . . ."

Taking the suggestion, the king did compare

した。まるで、きたならしいのです。それに、ごちそう
を食べて、ねてばかりいるので、ぶくぶく太ってしまい
ました。このあいだ作った、いいようふくも、ロボット
にはぴたりとあいますが、王さまには、きゅうくつです。

「ざんねんですが、王さま。こんどはロボットに行って
もらいましょう。かえってきたら、ロボットに話をきけ
ばいいじゃありませんか。」

「…………」

くやしいけれども、そうするより、しかたがありませ
んでした。

「もう、ねるぞ。」

王さまは、ベッドにもぐりこみました。しかし、ざん
ねんです。なんとかいいほうほうはないものか——。

外では、ロボットのおでかけのしたくがはじまりまし
た。じどうしゃをぴかぴかにみがきあげて、ついていく
へいたいたちも、そろったようです。

「そうだ。」王さまは、立ち上がりました。そして、窓か
ら、さけびました。

「おーい、待てっ。わしが行くぞ。いまから、おふろに
入って、とこやをして、きれいになって、行くぞっ、待っ
てくれ。」

himself with the robot. Yes, he was absolutely filthy. Also, all he'd been doing was eat lots of food and lie on his couch, so he'd become fat and flabby, and the good suit made a short while ago fitted the robot perfectly but was tight on him.

"It's a pity, Your Majesty, but perhaps we should let the robot go in your place this time. When he comes back you can hear all about it from him."

". . . . ."

The king felt hurt and angry, but there was nothing else that could be done.

"I'm going to bed."

The king crawled into bed. Still, what a pity. If there was only some way . . . .

Out in the courtyard, preparations were under way for the robot's departure. They were polishing the automobile until it sparkled, and the soldiers who would accompany the robot seemed all assembled.

"That's it!" The king jumped to his feet. He shouted from the window: "Hey, wait! *I* will go. I'll take a bath, shave, get all spiffed up, and be down in a jiffy. Wait for me!"

　なんてめずらしいことでしょう。

　王さまは、自分でおふろにとびこみました。そして、ごしごし、からだを洗いはじめました。

　ところが、いくら洗っても、きれいにならないのです。いくらながしても、きたないのです。

「たわしをもってこい。」

　たわしで洗って、やっと、あかがおちました。が、そのあとがたいへん。からだがひりひりいたくて、したぎがきられません。

「がまん、がまん。」

　それから、ひげそりです。

　大臣がやってきて、「王さま、はやくしないと、サーカスが、はじまってしまいますよ。」と、いそがせます。

「わかってる。いそいでやるから、もう少し待てっ。」

　王さまは、自分でカミソリをとって、のびたあごひげを、そりはじめました。

「はやく、はやく。」大臣が、また言うので、

「やかましいっ。」

　おこったとたん、だいじな口ひげのかたほうを、そりおとしてしまいました。

30

Now, wasn't that extraordinary!

He jumped into the bath, all on his own, and began scrubbing himself with a wash towel. He rubbed and rubbed, but he still couldn't get the dirt off. He poured and poured water over himself, but he was still dirty.

"Bring me a scrubbing brush!"

The dirt finally came off when he used a scrubbing brush. But with serious results. Now his skin stung him so much, it hurt something awful when he put on his underwear.

"Grin and bear it, grin and bear it . . . ."

Next was a shave. The chief minister came and hurried him up.

"Your Majesty, if you don't get ready quickly, the circus will begin."

"I know, I know! I'll be quick, give me a little more time!"

The king took the razor and started shaving his growth of whiskers by himself.

"Hurry, hurry!" said the chief minister again.

"Shut up!" shouted the king angrily — and in that instant shaved off one half of his precious moustache.

王さまが、いくら、ないてもさわいでも、ひげがかた
ほうきりないのでは、となりの国へ行くわけにはいきま
せん。

王さまは、さんざんでした。

ひげはかたほう、からだはひりひり……。しかたなく、
ベッドにもぐりこみましたが、こんどは、ねむれません。

王さまは、いつも、ごろごろねていたので、そうでな
くとも、ねむれないのです。ねむくないのです。朝まで、
ねむっていられないのです。ねむるのが、つらくなって
いました。

――さあ、もう、おきようかな――

そうおもいますが、おきるラッパは、七時にならない
と、なりません。

王さまは、かんがえました。

つぎの朝です。王さまは、五時ごろ、ロボットをおこ
しました。もっとも、ロボットですから、いつでも目を
さましています。

王さまは、ロボットに、何と言ったでしょう。こっそ
り聞いてみましょう。

32

Cry his heart out as he might, rant and rave as much as he pleased, there now was no way the king could go to the neighbor kingdom with half his moustache gone.

He felt utterly miserable.

Only half a moustache left, his skin stinging like mad, he crawled into bed. But now he couldn't sleep.

Even if he hadn't been feeling so terrible he still wouldn't be able to sleep, since he hadn't done anything but lounge about all day long. He wasn't sleepy. He lay in bed till morning, unable to sleep. Sleeping had become a chore.

(Oh well, guess I might as well get up . . . .) The thought passed through his mind, but the morning bugle would not sound until 7:00.

The king did some thinking.

The following morning, about 5:00, the king went to wake the robot. Naturally though, being a robot, it's always awake.

What do you think the king said to the robot? Let's eavesdrop.

「おい、ロボットくん。わしに、馬のりをおしえてくれよ。このごろ、うんどうをしないんで、太ってしまったんだ。」

王さまは、みんながねているときに、こっそり、馬のりをならいました。

つぎの朝になると、こんどは、

「おい、ロボットくん。わしに、べんきょうをおしえてくれよ。このごろ、なまけているんで、わすれそうなんだ。」

そして、まったくひさしぶりに、歯をみがくようになったということです。まったくひさしぶりに、しょくじの前に手を洗うようになったということです。それから、そのほか、王さまが、どういうふうにかわったかは、あなたがかんがえてください。おねがいします。

"I say, Robot, old chap, how about teaching me horseback riding? I haven't had much exercise lately, and I've put on some weight."

And so, while everyone else was still asleep, the king slipped out and had a lesson in horseback riding.

The next morning after that the king said to the robot: "I say, Robot, old chap, how about giving me some school lessons? I've been neglecting the books lately, and my memory's beginning to get rusty."

And the story goes that the king started brushing his teeth again, something he hadn't done for ages. And that he started washing his hands again before meals, something he hadn't done for ages. As for the rest of the ways the king changed, well, I'd be much obliged if you thought about them by yourself.

The Snow from Astra Yanko

TERAMURA Teruo

ヤンコ星の雪

❇

　王さまの話を、つづけます。寒がりで、よわむしの王さまです。

　王さまは、寒がりで、よわむしでしたから、シャツや洋服を、20まいも着ていました。それで、まるで雪だるまのように、まんまるに見えました。

「おお寒い。」

　王さまが、ふるえて、ちぢこまっているうちに、雪がふってきました。

　大臣が、王さまの部屋へ来て、言いました。

「王さま、雪がふってきました。外へ出て、雪がっせんをしましょう。暖かくなりますよ。」

　すると、王さまは、こんなことを言うのです。

「雪がつもってるのに、外へなんか出られるものか。＊からだがこおってしまうじゃないか。」

　大臣は、それでも、しんぱいなのです。

The Snow from Astra Yanko

❅

I'm going to tell you more about the king. He hated the cold, and he was a softy.

Because he hated the cold and was a softy, he wore about twenty layers of undershirts and clothes. As a result, he looked big and round, just like a snowman.

"Brr, it's cold!"

As the king huddled, shivering, it started to snow.

The chief minister came to the king's room and said, "Your Majesty, it has started to snow. Let's go outside and have a snowball fight. That'll warm you up!"

To this the king replied, "You think I can go outside when there's snow on the ground?!? I'll freeze!"

But the chief minister still was worried.

* ものか : a rhetorical question, implying the opposite is true.

「王さま。洋服をたくさん着て、ストーブにばかり当たっていては、体がよわくなってしまいますよ。」

「だって、寒いんだもの。」

「いけません。体がよわくなって、病気をすると、にがいくすりを飲まなくては、なりませんぞ。いたいちゅうしゃをしなくては、なりませんぞ。」

　王さま——好きなものは、玉子やき。きらいなものは、ちゅうしゃです。ちゅうしゃをされては、かないません。

「わかった。外へ出るよ。そのかわり、おしろの庭を、暖かくしてくれないか。」

「王さま。それはムリですよ。」

「庭に、いっぱいストーブを出したらいいじゃないか。うん、そうだ。庭のまわりを、ぐるっとストーブでかこむんだ。そうしよう、そうしよう。」

「王さま。それはムリですよ。今は、冬なんです。冬は、寒いにきまっているんですよ。」

「それじゃあ、はやく、春をつれて来い。」

「王さま。それはムリですよ。春の小鳥はねむっているし、チューリップは、まだ芽も出していません。桜のつぼみもありません。」

「なあに、かまうものか。さあ、へいたいたちに言い付

"Your Majesty, if you just put on a lot of clothes and sit there by the stove all the time, your health will deteriorate."

"I'm doing it because I'm *cold*!"

"But you mustn't. If your health deteriorates and you get sick, you will have to drink some bitter medicine. And you will have to get painful injections."

Now, what the king liked most were omelettes, and what he hated most were injections. He couldn't stand being given an injection.

"All right, all right! I'll go outside. But then you have to warm up the palace garden for me."

"That can't be done, Your Majesty."

"You can put a lot of heaters out in the garden, can't you? Yes, that's it! Circle the whole garden with a ring of heaters. That's what we'll do!"

"Your Majesty. It can't be done. It's winter now. Winter is meant to be cold."

"In that case, hurry up and bring on spring."

"Your Majesty, it can't be done. The birds of spring are still asleep, for one thing, and the tulips still haven't even put out their buds. There aren't any buds on the cherry trees, either."

"Who cares? Go on, order the soldiers to get

けて、まず、庭の雪をどけるんだ。そして、そのあとに、つくりもののチューリップをうえて、紙の花を桜の木にはり付けて、おしろでかっている小鳥を、＊　庭にはなすんだ。」

「王さま。それはムリですよ。」

「うるさい。」

　言い出したらきかない王さまです。大臣は、しかたなく、王さまの言うとおりにしました。

　へいたいが、おしろの庭の雪かきをはじめました。王さまは、窓から、庭をながめて言いました。

「みんなで、雪だるまを作るんだ。雪がなくなるまで、いくつもいくつも、作るんだ。」

　雪だるまが324個もできました。雪だるまは、庭のすみに、ぎょうぎよく並んでいました。

　王さまの言い付けどおり、ビニールのチューリップがうえられました。紙の花が、桜の木にはり付けられました。おしろでかっている小鳥が、庭にはなされました。

「さあ、これで、春が来るだろう。」

　王さまは、そろりそろりと、庭へ出てみました。

　ところが、そのとたん、北風が、

　　　びゅう　　るるる

rid of the snow from the garden first. After that they are to plant artificial tulips, glue paper flowers to the cherry trees, and then release into the garden all the birds we keep in the palace."

"Your Majesty, you're asking the impossible!"

"Quiet!!"

Once the king has said something he won't budge. Helplessly, the chief minister did as the king said.

The soldiers started shovelling away the snow in the palace garden. The king was watching from his window. "All of you," he said, "are to make snowmen! You are to make snowman after snowman, until all the snow is gone!"

They made 324 snowmen. The snowmen stood in neat rows, row upon row, in one corner of the garden.

As the king had commanded, vinyl tulips were planted. Paper flowers were glued to the cherry trees. All the birds kept in the palace were released into the garden.

"Well now, this should bring on spring," said the king, as he slowly, very slowly, went out into the garden.

But no sooner was the king outside than the North Wind came along, whistling and howling,

---

* かっている : from かう "raise or keep (an animal)," not to be confused with the word for "buy."

　　　びゅーん　んん

と吹いてきて、王さまは、ふきとばされてしまいました。
洋服をたくさん着て、ボールのような王さまは、ころこ
ろところがって、雪だるまにぶつかって、やっととまり
ました。

「うへっ。寒いぞ。」

　見ると、桜の木にはり付けた紙の花が、ひらひらとび
まわっています。花が、風に吹かれて、どこかへきえた
とき、こんどは、また、雪がふってきました。

「たすけてくれえ。」

　王さまは、また、ころがるようにして、部屋へかえっ
てきました。

　小鳥たちは、もっと暖かい国を見つけに、とんでいっ
てしまいました。チューリップは、雪をかぶって、まっ
白になってしまいました。

　　　　　　　　☃　☃

　寒がりで、よわむしの王さまは、考えました。

「ようし、こうなれば、ゆげのような暖かい風を吹かせ
て、わたのように暖かい雪をふらせなくてはダメだ。な

44

and the king was sent flying. Dressed in so many layers of clothes that he resembled a round ball, the king went rolling along and finally came to a stop only when he bumped into a snowman.

"Yow! It's freezing out here!"

Then he saw the paper flowers that had been glued onto the cherry trees, flying about everywhere. When the wind blew them out of sight, the snow started falling again.

"Help me-e-e, somebody!!"

The king stumbled back to his room.

The birds flew away in search of a warmer land. The tulips, covered in snow, were all white.

Our cold-hater and softy of a king did some thinking.

"All right, if this is how things are, we need to have a wind blow that's warm, sort of like steam, and a snow come down that's as warm as cotton.

にか、いいほうほうはないものか。」

　そこで、おしろのとしょしつへ行って、いろいろと本をしらべました。

（王さまが、自分でべんきょうするなんて、あなたは、聞いたことがありましたっけ）

〈雪の本〉を見ると、雪は、ヤンコ星の工場で作られ、ジェットポンプで、雲におくられる——、と書いてありました。

　王さまは、すぐに大臣をよびました。

「おい、大臣。ヤンコ星へ行く、ロケットをよういしろ。わしは、ヤンコ星の王さまにあって、暖かい雪をふらせるように、たのんで来る。」

「王さま。それはムリです。雪は、もともと冷たいものなのです。氷のつぶのようなものなのです。」

「いや、わたのように、暖かい雪だって、作れるはずだ。」

「そんなことありませんよ。もし、雪が暖かくなれば、ストーブは冷たくなるでしょう。洋服を着たら、寒くなるでしょう。さかさまですよ。」

「さかさまでも、かまわん。」

「こまったなあ。」

「こまってないで、大臣は、はやくロケットをよういす

There must be some good way to . . . ."

He went to the palace library and looked around in some books. (Have you ever heard of that before? The king studying without anybody forcing him!)

He looked through a book called *The Book of Snow*, and there it said that snow was made in the factories of Astra Yanko, from which it was sent by means of jet pumps to the clouds.

The king called for the chief minister at once.

"Chief Minister, old chap, I am going to Astra Yanko. Prepare the rocket ship. I am going to meet the king of Astra Yanko and ask him to have warm snow fall."

"Your Majesty. It can't be done. By its very nature snow is cold. It's sort of like tiny droplets of ice, is what it is."

"No, it should also be possible to make snow that's warm, like cotton."

"No it isn't possible! If snow became warm, then heaters would be cold. And when you put on clothes you would feel colder. Everything would be topsy-turvy."

"Who cares if it *is* topsy-turvy?"

"Oh, for heaven's sake!"

"Don't stand there for-heaven's-saking me,

ればいいんだ。」

　さあ、たいへんです。

　王さまをのせたロケットが、だだあーんと、ヤンコ星
めがけて飛んでいきました。

　そして、まあまあ、うまいぐあいに、ヤンコ星の雪の
工場につきました。

　王さまは、ヤンコ星の王さまに、会いました。

「やあ、雪の王さま。あなたがふらせる雪は、冷たくて
いけません。もっと、暖かくて、わたのようにふんわり
したのを、ふらせてくださいよ。」

「これはこれは、みょうなたのみですな。あいにく、わ
たしの工場では、冷たいのしか作っておりませんので
ね。それに、雪は、冷たいのがあたりまえですよ。」

「そこを、なんとか、考えて……」

「できませんな。」

「冷たいのを、暖めるだけで、いいんでしょう。」

「あなたは、さかさまがお好きなようですな。あはははは
は。」

　とうとう、王さまのねがいは、聞きとどけられません
でした。しかたなく、王さまは、またロケットにのって、

48

you should be preparing the rocket ship, pronto!"

The chief minister had a real job on his hands.

The rocket ship, with the king aboard, blasted off, heading for Astra Yanko.

And, surprise, surprise, luckily it arrived at the snow factories of Astra Yanko.

The king met the king of Astra Yanko.

"Greetings, Snow King. The snow you are dropping is cold. Cold is no good. I'd like you to drop something warmer, something nice and fluffy, like cotton."

"Well, well, isn't this a curious request! Unfortunately, in my factories all we make is cold snow. Besides, snow is meant to be cold, in case you didn't know."

"You can think of some way to remedy that, I'm . . . ."

"No I can't."

"Maybe you could just warm up some of the cold snow before . . . ."

"You seem to like having things topsy-turvy, eh? A-ha-ha-ha-ha!"

In the end, the king's request was not granted. There was nothing the king could do but board

かえります。

　ところが、です。

　ロケットが飛び出して、ヤンコ星の、雪の王さまが
「さようなら」と手をふったとき、ロケットが、ぶるぶ
るっとふるえ出しました。まるで、寒がりで、よわむし
の王さまのようにです。

　ロケットは、こんどは、ぐるぐると回り出しました。
「しまった、こしょうだ。」運転手が、さけびました。

　ロケットは、それでも、しばらくしてこしょうがなおっ
たようです。ふるえも、とまりました。が──気が付く
と、おかしなことに、ロケットがうしろむきにすすんで
いるのです。そして、王さまの体が、ほかほかと、暖か
くなってきました。暖かく、暖かく、しまいには、あつ
くさえなってきました。おもたいうちゅう服など、着て
いるのが、つらくなりました。

「わしは、うちゅう服を、ぬぐぞっ。」王さまが言いまし
た。

「王さま。なにをおっしゃるのですか。ここでうちゅう
服をぬいだら、体が、はれつしてしまいます。」運転手が、
とめます。

「でも、わしは、あつくてしかたがないんだ。」

50

his rocket ship and go home.

But . . . .

As the rocket ship lifted off and the snow king of Astra Yanko waved good-bye, the rocket ship began shivering. Just the same way that our cold-hating, softy king shivered.

Next, the rocket ship started spinning.

"Darn! A malfunction!" shouted the pilot.

Yet after a short while the malfunction seemed to be corrected. The shivering stopped, too.

But then they noticed something strange: the rocket ship was not facing forwards as it went through space, but backwards! Also, the king's body began to get very warm. Then warmer, even warmer, until finally it even became hot. Wearing the heavy space suit grew unbearable.

"I'm going to take off this space suit," he said.

The pilot stopped him. "Your Majesty, what are you talking about? If you take your space suit off now, your body will burst into pieces."

"But I can't stand it, it's so hot!"

「もう少し、待ってください。地球に近づいたら、ぬい
でもいいですよ。」

「はやくしろ。スピード、スピード。」

　王さまは、がまんできずに、

「まだか、まだか。」と言いつづけました。

　運転手にとっては、そんなことより、さかさまに飛ん
でいるロケットのほうがしんぱいなのです。

　ロケットは、それでも、まあまあ、うまいぐあいに、
おしろにかえってきました。

「おかえりなさあい。」と、むかえた人たちの前に、王さ
まが、ロケットからおりてきました。

　そのすがたを見た人たちは、

「あっ。」

　おどろきました。

　はだかの王さまが、逆立ちでおりてきたのです。

　　　　　　　　　　👲 ❄ 👲

　寒がりで、よわむしの王さまが、まるでさかさまにな
りました。

　歩くのが、さかさま。

"Wait just a little longer. When we get close to earth it'll be safe to take it off."

"Then hurry up! Give her more speed — *speed*, man!!"

Unable to stand it, the king kept saying, "Still not there? Still not there?"

The pilot had something more important to worry about: the rocket ship flying back-to-front.

Despite everything, with a bit of luck the rocket ship managed to get back to the palace.

In full view of the people who came to greet him with shouts of "Welcome back, Your Majesty!" the king disembarked from the rocket ship.

When the people saw him they all gasped. They couldn't believe their eyes. There was the king, in his undershorts, coming down the stairway walking on his hands.

☃ ❄ ☃

The cold-hating, softy of a king was now completely topsy-turvy.

He walked on his hands.

冬なのに、はだか。

「ああ、あついな。もっと、寒くならないかな。」部屋の中に、氷のはしらを20本も立てて、氷の入ったおふろに、つかっているのです。＊　それでも、あついので、外へ出ました。

　もちろん、逆立ちで、おしろの庭を歩いていきます。庭のすみに、あの、雪だるまが並んでいました。

「おい、雪だるまくん、あそぼうや。わしは、きみが大好きだ。」

　ところが、体のあつい王さまがさわると、雪だるまが、とろんと、とろけてしまいました。

「や、なんで、わしをきらうんだ。そのままで、あそんでくれよ。」

　いけません。とろん、とろんと、とけてしまうのです。そして、あとに、わたくずのような、小さな雪だるまの人形がのこりました。

「……？……」

　つぎの雪だるまも、そうでした。

　　　　　とろん

「ああ、冷たいものがほしい。ね、雪だるまくん。きえないで、わしをだいてくれ。」

54

Though it was midwinter, he went around in his undershorts.

"Golly it's hot! I wish it would get colder!"

Twenty pillars of ice had been set up in his room, and he himself sat soaking in a bathtub filled with ice. Still feeling hot, he went outside. He went walking about the palace garden . . . on his hands, of course. In one corner of the garden stood those 324 snowmen.

"I say, Snowman, old boy, let's play a game. I'm quite fond of you."

But when the king's hot body touched the snowman, it started melting away: drip, drip.

"Hey, how come you don't like me? Stay the way you are and let's play."

It was useless. The snowman kept on melting. In the end all that was left was a tiny snowman doll that looked like a small wad of cotton.

". . . ? . . ."

The same thing happened to the next snowman the king touched: drip, drip.

"Gee, I need something cold. Listen, Snowman, don't disappear on me, give me a hug."

* つかっている : from つかる "soak," "be immersed in"; cf. つける "soak, steep; pickle" (whence つけもの).

55

とろん　　　とろん　　　とろん

324個の雪だるまが、みなとろけて、小さな人形になってしまいました。

王さまは、とうとう、氷のはった池に、飛びこみました。

すると、じゅーっと、おとがして、水が暖かくなっていきました。10センチも、あつくはっていた氷が、＊10分たたないうちに、＊＊　とけてしまったのです。よほど、体があつかったんですね。

王さまは、それでも、はじめのうちは、気持ちよさそうにおよいでいました。手や足をばたばたさせると、足のほうへ、すすむのです。さかさまなのです。

そのうちに、池から、ゆげが立ってきました。

大臣がやってきて、王さまに言いました。

「王さま。はやく上がってください。池のさかなが、にえてしまいます。」

「やかましい。」

王さまは、池から上がりました。いつまでも池にいたら、あつくてたまらないからです。

そのとき、雲が、ぽっかりとわれて、太陽が出ました。

おしろの庭が、ぱあーっと、あかるくなりました。風

Drip, drip; drip, drip; drip, drip.

One after another, 324 snowmen melted down and turned into small dolls.

Finally the king jumped into the pond, over which lay a sheet of ice.

When the king landed in the pond, there was a loud hiss, and the water started warming up. There had been a layer of ice about four inches thick, but in less than ten minutes the ice was melted. The king's body had been very hot indeed.

Even so, at first the king enjoyed a pleasant swim. When he paddled with his arms and legs, instead of going forward he went backwards. That's because everything was topsy-turvy for him.

Before long, steam started rising from the pond.

The chief minister came up and said to the king: "Your Majesty, please come out of the pond at once. The fish in the pond will all be boiled."

"Stop nagging!!"

The king came out of the pond. If he stayed in it too long, he'd get terribly hot again.

Just then there was a break in the clouds and the sun came out. The palace garden blazed into

---

* あつく : "thickly"; not to be confused with the word for "hot."

** たたない : from たつ "elapse, pass."

もやんで、やっと、暖かくなったのです。

　ところが、王さまは、どうでしょう。

「やれやれ、やっと、少し、すずしくなった。」と言って、

日当りのいい所で、よこになりました。

「それでは、みんな。おやすみ。」

　おやおや。王さまは、なにか、まちがっているようで

す。太陽が出たので、夜になったと思ったんですね。

　そうとは気が付かない大臣は、

「王さま、そんな所でねていては、かぜをひきますよ。」

　王さまをつれていこうとするのですが、おきようとも

しません。

「そうか、王さまは、さかさまになったんだな。」

　そう気が付きましたが、みょうなことに、なったもの

です。＊

　王さまは、暖かい日当りで、いや、すずしい日当り？

で、ぐっすりとねむってしまいました。

☃ ❄ ❄ ☃

　夜になりました。

　王さまは、「やあ、また、あつくなってきたな。」と言っ

sunshine. The wind stopped, and at last the air felt warm.

How did the king react, though?

"What a relief! At last it has cooled off a bit!" he said, and he lay down where he could catch the full rays of the sun.

"All right, everybody, good night!"

What's this? It looks like the king's making some mistake. Aha, the sun came out, so he thought it was nighttime.

But the chief minister doesn't realize this, and he says to him, "Your Majesty, if you sleep there you'll catch cold." He tries to lead the king away, but the king won't even get up.

"Ha haa, I see. The king's all topsy-turvy," the chief minister realized. What strange things were going on!

In the warm rays of the sun — or should we say, the cool rays of the sun? — the king fell sound asleep.

☃ ❆ ❆ ☃

Night fell.

"Gosh, it's hot again," the king said, rising to

---

* ものです : here, shows wonderment.

て、起き上がりました。ほんとうは、雪でぬれたじめん
が、かちん　かちんに　こおっているのです。
「そろそろ、起きようか。」
　さてさて、こまったことです。
　すると、庭のすみにあった、雪だるまの人形が、ごそ
ごそうごき出しました。歌を歌っているのです。

　　　とっとこ　　どどっこ　　ふいーっ
　　　逆立ち王さま　　あっはっはっ
　　　お日さましずんで　朝が来た
　　　ラッパがなったら　　しずかだな
　　　おゆが　冷たく　わいてるぞ
　　　ごはんの前に　　足洗え
　　　病気になったら　飛び歩け
　　　とっとこ　　どどっこ　　ふいー　　ふいーっ

　歌いながら、おどりながら、人形が、一列に並びまし
た。そして、どどっこ　とっとこ、ひとつにかたまりま
した。まだ、歌はやめません。ぐるぐるぐるぐる回って
いるうちに、まるで、雪のかたまりのようになりました。
　すると、そのかたまりが、

60

his feet. As a matter of fact, though, the snow-moistened ground had a thin coat of ice, which crackled underfoot.

"Guess I might as well get up."

(My oh my, how mixed up can you get?)

At this point, the snowmen dolls in the corner of the garden rustled and shuffled and stirred into life. They were singing a song.

Wobbledy hobbledy ho!

Ol' topsy-turvy king, ho ho!

When the sun sets, "Oh it's morning!"

When the bugle blows, "Quiet, isn't it?"

When the bath water's cold, "It's boiling!"

Before sitting to eat, he washes his feet,

And when he gets sick, he's up and about.

Wobbledy hobbledy ho-ho!

As they sang and danced, the dolls formed a line. Then, with a wobbledy hobbledy, they merged into one. Without a pause in their singing they spun round and round like a top, in the course of which they formed into a solid ball of snow.

When this happened, the solid ball of snow

　　　　　どどっこ

と、はれつして、そこに、ヤンコ星の、雪の王さまが立っ
ていました。

「あはははは。」

　雪の王さまがわらうと、北風が、つよく吹きあれました
た。

　　　　びゅう　るるる

　　　　　　びゅーん　んん

　雪の王さまが言いました。

「やあ、王さま。このあいだは、しつれいしました。逆
立ちとは、いいかっこうですな。さかさまなことがお好
きだから、いいでしょう。」

「…………」

「さて、わたしは、ここにいた、わたしの子供たちをつ
れて、ヤンコ星へ帰りましょう。では、さようなら。」

「待ってくれ。」王さまは、さけびました。

「待ってくださいよ。雪の王さま。わしは、あつくてしょ
うがない。ヤンコ星に帰ったら、もっと冷たい雪をこし
らえて、ふらせてください。なにしろ、あつくて、かな
わんのだ。」

　すると、また、どこからか、

burst open with a boom, and standing there was the Snow King of Astra Yanko.

"A-ha-ha-ha-ha!"

When the Snow King laughed, the North Wind blew mightily, whistling and howling like mad.

Then the Snow King spoke. "Greetings, Your Majesty. Sorry for being rude the other day. You cut quite a nice figure, standing on your hands. Since you're so fond of topsy-turvy things, I suppose you don't mind."

". . . . . ."

"Well, I just thought I would collect my children from here and take them back to Astra Yanko. Be seeing you."

"Wait!" shouted the king. "Please wait, Snow King Your Majesty. I'm so hot, so terribly hot! When you return to Astra Yanko, please make some colder snow and let it fall on us. Y'see, I can't take this heat."

Whereupon, from somewhere came the sound

　　　とっとこ　どどっこ　ふいーっ　ふいーっ

　歌が聞こえたとみるまに、ヤンコ星の王さまが、きゅうに大声で、言いました。

「かってなことを言うな。わたしは、しらんぞっ。」

　おしろがゆれるような、大声でした。王さまは、びっくりして、ひっくりかえってしまいました。

　つまり、もとのように、ちゃんと立ってしまったのです。すると、体も、もとどおりになって、寒くなってきました。なにしろ、はだかなんですからね。

　　　「はっくしょんー。」

大きなくしゃみをひとつ。気が付くと、ヤンコ星の雪王さまは、どこにもいません。王さまのくしゃみにのって、ヤンコ星へ帰ってしまったのです。

　そして、王さまのねがいだけは聞きとどけてくれたのでしょう。冷たい雪が、おしろにもふってきました。

of the song "Wobbledy hobbledy, ho! ho!" once again, and the king of Astra Yanko suddenly boomed out: "Stop wanting everything your own way! I won't be responsible for what happens."

His voice boomed so loud the palace shook. The king was so surprised he did a flip.

That is to say, he was standing on his two legs again, the way he was supposed to. His body, too, had returned to normal, and he was feeling cold again. And no wonder—he had only his undershorts on, remember?

"A-TCHOO!" He sneezed a mighty sneeze.

When he looked around, the Snow King from Astra Yanko was nowhere to be seen. He had returned to Astra Yanko riding on the king's sneeze.

But the one thing the Snow King did seem to do was grant the king his wish, for now cold snow started falling upon the palace the same as everywhere else.